READING/WRITING COMPANION

Mc
Graw
Hill
Education

Cover: Nathan Love, Erwin Madrid

mheducation.com/prek-12

Send all inquiries to:
McGraw-Hill Education
Two Penn Plaza
New York, NY 10121

ISBN: 978-0-07-902057-4
MHID: 0-07-902057-7

Printed in the United States of America.

4 5 6 7 8 9 LMN 23 22 21 20   C

Welcome to Wonders!

Explore exciting **Literature**, **Science**, and **Social Studies** texts!

★ **READ** about the world around you!

★ **THINK**, **SPEAK**, and **WRITE** about genres!

★ **COLLABORATE** in discussions and inquiry!

★ **EXPRESS** yourself!

my.mheducation.com

Use your student login to read texts and practice phonics, spelling, grammar, and more!

Unit 6 Weather for All Seasons

The Big Idea

How do weather and seasons affect us?

Week 1 • The Four Seasons

Digital Tools Find this eBook and other resources at: my.mheducation.com

Week 2 • What's the Weather?

Week 3 • Stormy Weather

Writing and Grammar

Wrap Up Units 5 and 6

Weather for All Seasons

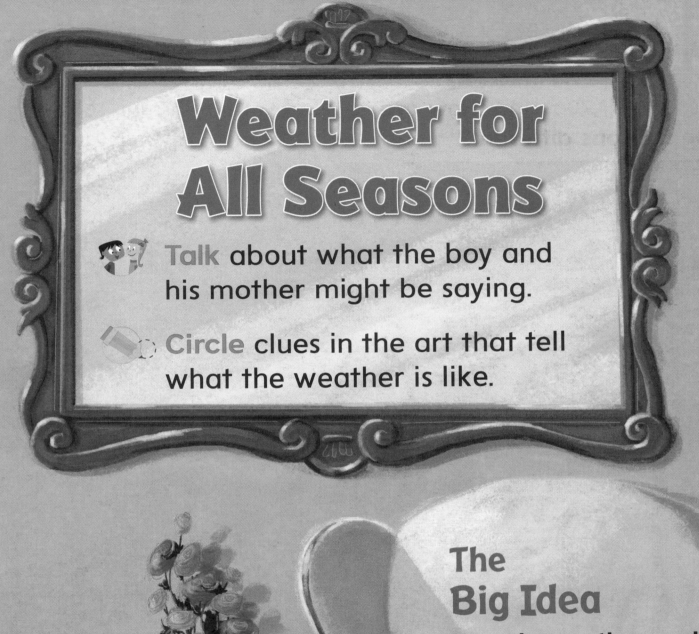

Talk about what the boy and his mother might be saying.

Circle clues in the art that tell what the weather is like.

The Big Idea

How do weather and seasons affect us?

Talk About It

Talk about the season in the photo.

 Write the name of the season in the top oval. Then write words that tell about this season in the other ovals.

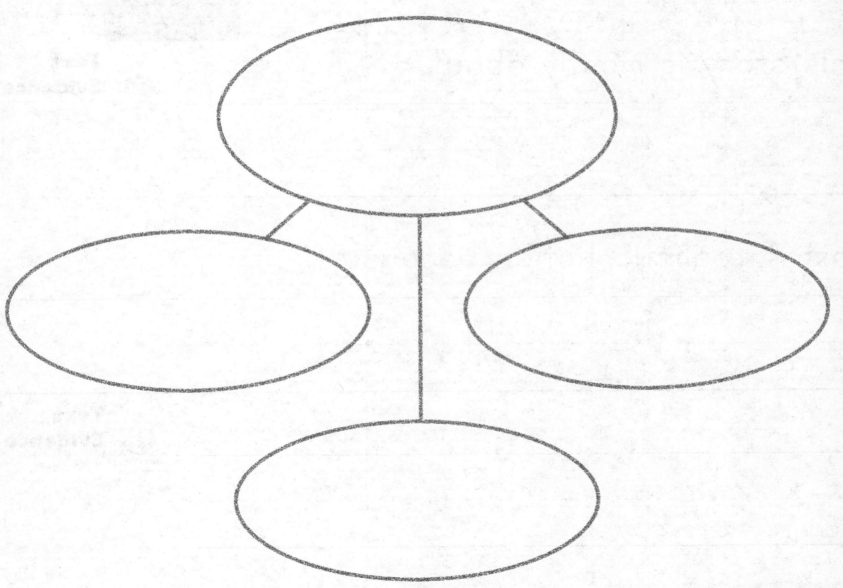

Ariel Skelley/Blend Images/Getty Images

Retell the realistic fiction story.

 Write about the story.

This story is mostly about

_____

- -

_____

Text Evidence

Page

This is realistic fiction because

_____

- -

_____

 Text Evidence

Page

Talk about how you can tell that summer is coming.

 Draw and **write** about one way you can tell that summer is coming.

Summer is coming when

The events in a story are the plot.
An author tells the plot in a certain order,
or sequence. Words such as <u>first</u>, <u>next</u>,
and <u>last</u> tell the order.

 Listen to part of the story.

 Talk about what happens **first**, **next**,
and **last**.

 Draw what happens.

First

Next

Last

Look at pages 26–27.

 Talk about how the words and pictures show what season it is.

 Draw or **list** clues.

When trees bloom, it is

Listen to page 31.

 Talk about the words that help you picture what summer is like.

 Draw a picture and **write** the words.

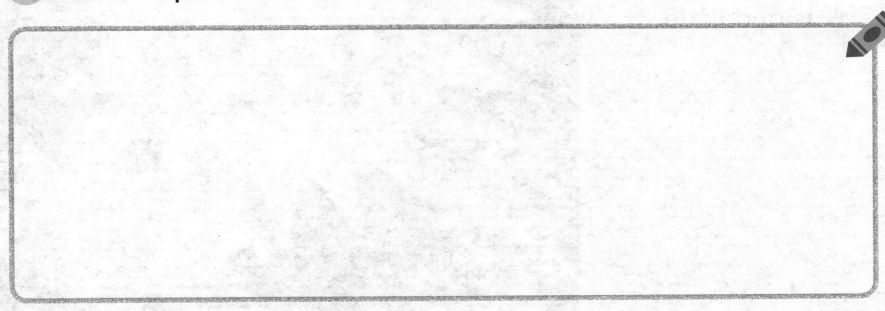

Summer is

_____

- -

_____

Find Text Evidence

 Read to find out what is hot.

 Circle the words **is** and **little**.

Is It Hot?

Ed Bock/Corbis/Getty Images

Ben is a little cat.

It is a bit hot.

🔍 **Find Text Evidence**

○ **Circle** the object whose name begins with the same sound as **bed**.

Underline the word that ends with the same sound as **lab**.

It is hot, hot, hot.

We see a fin!

Deb can hit with a bat.

Deb can hit a lot!

Shared Read

🔍 **Find Text Evidence**

⬡ **Circle** words that begin with the same sound as **lid**.

⬡ **Underline** words that rhyme.

Let Rob sip, sip, sip!

Leander Baerenz/Digital Vision/Getty Images

Lin is not a bit hot.

Lin can hop on top!

Shared Read

🔍 **Find Text Evidence**

Circle what is on top.

Retell the text. Make pictures in your mind to help you.

A red hat is on it.

I set the hat on top.

It is not a bit hot!

Hop a lot if it is not hot!

Listen to the poem. Look at the picture. What season is the poet writing about?

Quick Tip

When we read, we can make pictures in our mind. This helps us better understand what we read.

 Talk about what a "flying pool" is. How do you know?

 Circle the flying pool.

Talk about the words in the poem. Which words tell what the poet likes about summer?

 Write and **draw** the words.

Words	Pictures

Talk About It

What does the poet not like about summer? Which words tell you? Use the words to make a picture in your mind.

Research and Inquiry

Research a Season

Step 1 **Talk** about the different seasons.
Choose one to learn about.

Step 2 **Write** a question about this season.

_____

- -

_____

_____

- -

_____

Step 3 **Look** at books or use the Internet.
Look up words you do not know.
Use a picture dictionary.

Step 4 Draw **and** write **about what you learned.**

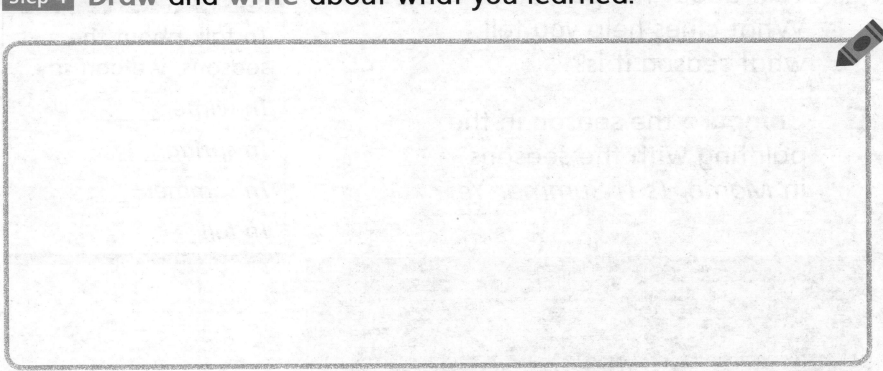

I learned

_____

- -

_____

Step 5 Choose **a good way to present your work.**

Make Connections

 Talk about the painting. What clues help you tell what season it is?

 Compare the season in the painting with the seasons in *Mama, Is It Summer Yet?*

Quick Tip

To talk about the seasons, we can say:

In winter ___.

In spring ___.

In summer ___.

In fall ___.

image courtesy National Gallery of Art

What I Know Now

Think about the texts you read this week.

The texts tell about

_____

- -

_____

_____

- -

_____

 Think about what you learned this week.
What else would you like to learn?
Talk about your ideas.

 Share one thing you learned about
realistic fiction stories.

Talk About It

Essential Question What happens in different kinds of weather?

Talk about the weather in this photo. What is the girl doing?

Draw and **write** about something you can do in this kind of weather.

On a rainy day, I can

_ _

Retell the fantasy story.

 Write about the fantasy.

This fantasy is about

_____

- -

_____

 Text Evidence

Page

This is a fantasy because

_____

- -

_____

- -

_____

Text Evidence

Page

Talk about how you can tell the weather will change.

 Draw and **write** about one way.

The weather will change when

_____

- -

_____

An author tells the plot of a story in sequence. Words such as <u>first</u>, <u>next</u>, and <u>last</u> tell the order.

 Listen to part of the story.

 Talk about what happens **first**, **next**, and **last**.

 Draw what happens.

First

Next

Last

 Look at the colors the illustrator uses on pages 12–13.

 Talk about why the illustrator uses these colors. Think about how they help you understand the weather.

 Write your ideas.

_____

- -

_____

_____

- -

_____

_____

- -

_____

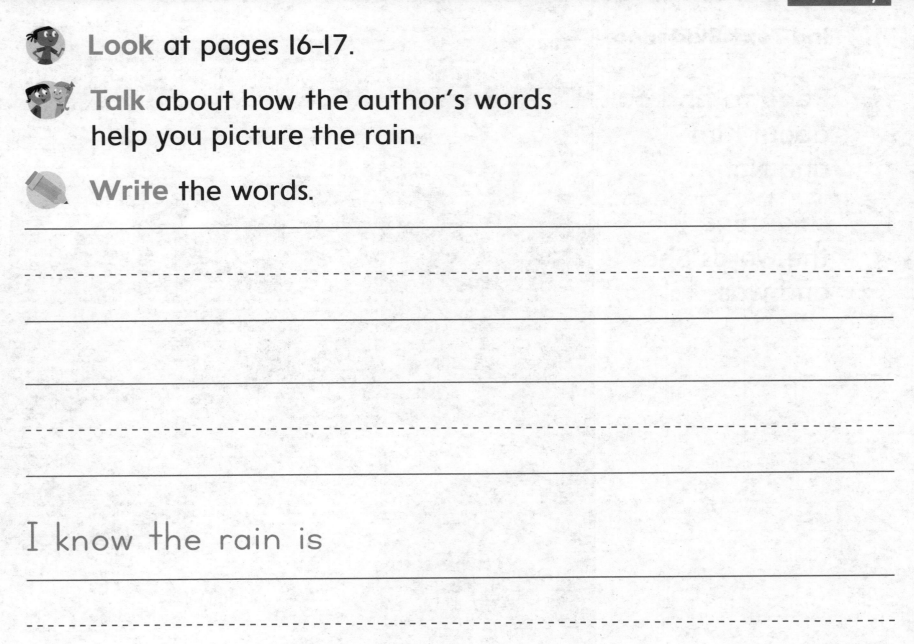

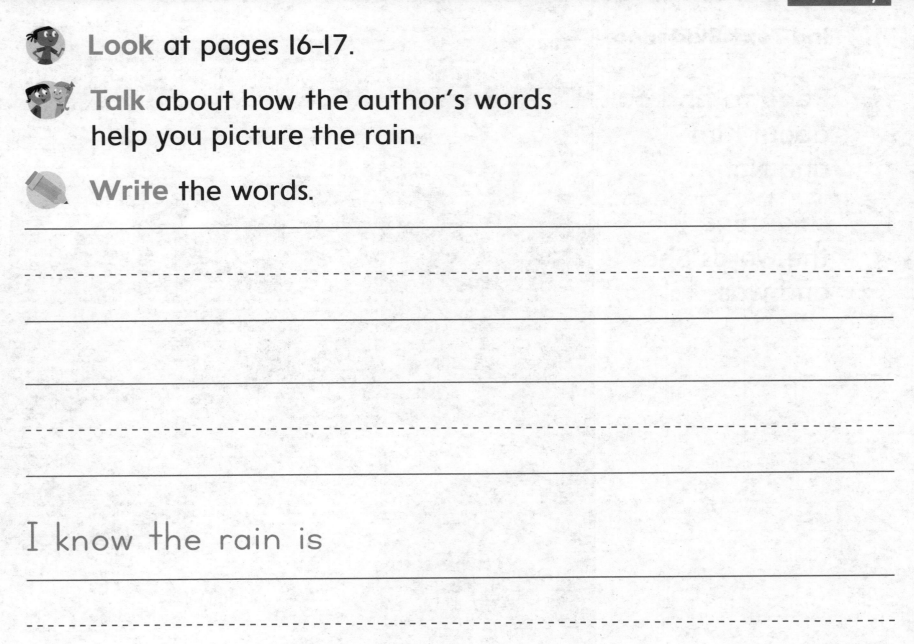 **Look** at pages 16–17.

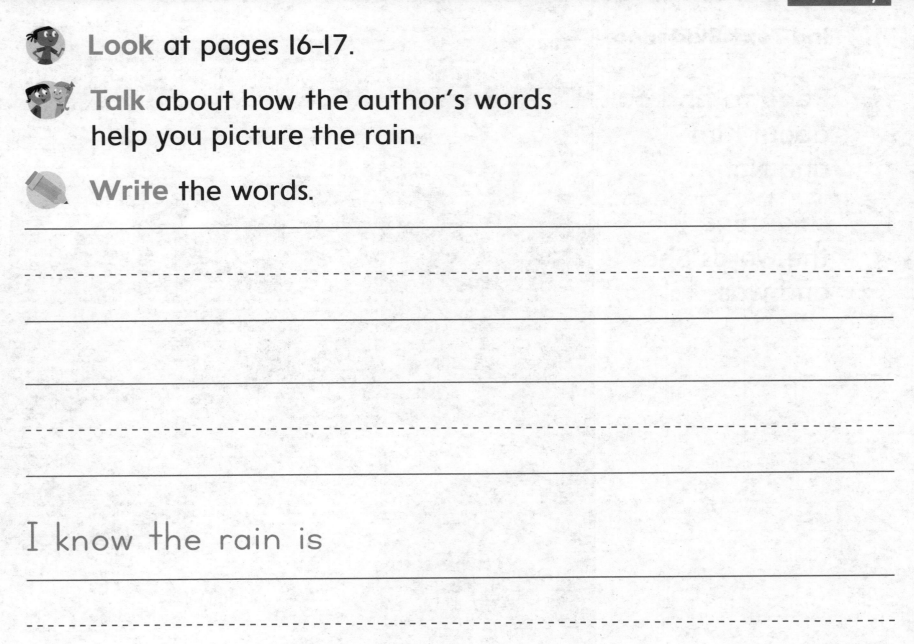 **Talk** about how the author's words help you picture the rain.

 Write the words.

_____

- - - - - - - - - - - - - - - - - - - -

_____

_____

- - - - - - - - - - - - - - - - - - - -

_____

I know the rain is

_____

- - - - - - - - - - - - - - - - - - - -

_____

Find Text Evidence

 Read to find out about Kim and Nan.

 Underline the words **She** and **was**.

Kim and Nan

Kim had a lot to pack.

She was a kid on the go.

Shared Read

📖 **Read** and point to the spaces between words in each sentence.

🖼️ **Circle** who sat on a little rock.

Nan sat on a big rock.

Kim sat on a little rock.

Kim was hot, hot, hot.

Kim had to sip a bit.

Shared Read

 **Find Text Evidence**

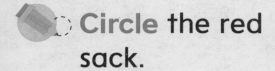 **Circle** the red sack.

Talk about how Nan and Kim feel on page 43. What clues help you to know?

Kim had a red sack.

Kim fed a lot.

Nan and Kim sat and sat.

It was not a bit hot!

Shared Read

 Find Text Evidence

 Think about what Kim is thinking on page 45. Make a picture in your mind.

Retell the story. Tell what happens in order.

Kim ran back.

Nan ran back.

Kim has a red pack.

Kim is a kid on the go!

Look at the pictures and words. How does the author tell about the weather?

TUESDAY

It's cloudy, but there is no rain.

WEDNESDAY

Those dark clouds bring rain and storms.

 Read the speech bubbles.

 Talk about the weather information they tell.

 Circle the words in each speech bubble that give clues.

Quick Tip

Speech bubbles tell what characters are saying.

Look at the label on each picture.

 Talk about what information the labels tell.

 Write about this information.

On Tuesday, there is

_____

- -

_____

On Wednesday, there is

_____

- -

_____

Talk About It

Why do you think the title of this text is "Cloud Watch"? How do the speech bubbles, labels, and pictures tell about the weather?

Research the Weather

Step 1 Talk about different kinds of weather.
Choose one kind of weather to learn about.

Step 2 Write a question about this kind
of weather.

_____

- -

_____

_____

- -

_____

Step 3 Look at books or use the Internet.
Look up words you do not know.
Use a picture dictionary.

Step 4 Draw **and** write **about what you learned.**

- -

Step 5 Choose **a good way to present your work.**

Integrate | Make Connections

 Talk about the photo. What clues help you tell what the weather is like?

 Compare the weather in this photo with the weather in *Rain*.

Quick Tip

We can talk about hot weather using these words:

heat wave, hot spell, muggy, summery, sunny, warm

Ariel Skelley/Blend Images LLC

50 Unit 6 · Week 2

What I Know Now

Think about the texts you read this week.

The texts tell about

_____

- -

_____

_____

- -

_____

 Think about what you learned this week.
What else would you like to learn?
Talk about your ideas.

 Share one thing you learned
about fantasy stories.

Talk About It

Essential Question How can you stay safe in bad weather?

Talk about the photo. How can you describe this weather?

 SCIENCE

Draw and **write** about how you can stay safe in this kind of weather.

In this weather, I can

_____

- -

_____

Retell the realistic fiction story.

 Write about the story.

This story is mostly about

 Text Evidence

Page

This is realistic fiction because

Text Evidence

Page

Talk about stormy weather you
have seen. How did it make you feel?

 Draw and **write** about what
this stormy weather was like.

An author tells the **plot** of a story
in a certain order, or **sequence**.

 Listen to part of the story.

 Talk about what happens **first**, **next**, and **last**.

 Write about what happens.

First

Next

Last

 Listen to pages 5-7. Look at how the words are shown on these pages.

 Talk about why the author uses different kinds of type.

 Write about how this helps you to better understand the story.

Using different kinds of type helps me

_____

_____

_____

_____

Listen to pages 26–27.

 Talk about how the girl feels about the storm now. What clues does the author give in the words and picture?

 Draw how the girl feels now.

Make Inferences

In this story, the mother talks to her daughter about the storm using rhyming language. Why do you think the author wrote the story this way?

🔍 **Find Text Evidence**

👩 Read to find out about Mack and Ben.

🔶 Circle a word that begins with the same sounds as **sled**.

Mack and Ben

Pit, pat, pit, pat, pit, pat!

Mack ran with Ben.

He did not slip.

Find Text Evidence

 Think about what Mack might be thinking. Make a picture in your mind.

 Underline words that begin with the same sound as **he**.

Mack was a bit sad.

Ben hid in a little bed.

Mom fed Mack and Ben.

She had a hot, hot ham.

Find Text Evidence

Circle a picture whose name begins with the same sounds as **clip**.

Underline words that end with the same sound as **rock**.

The clock can tick, tock!

Mack and Ben sat and sat.

Mack did not hit.

He did not kick.

Shared Read

 **Find Text Evidence**

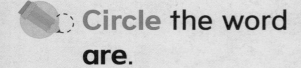 **Circle** the word **are**.

Retell the story. Were there parts you did not understand? Use the words and pictures to help you.

Ben can pack a bag.

Mack can pack a tan bat.

Mack can clap.

Mack and Ben are back!

Look at the photos. What clues tell you that a storm is coming?

Whoosh! In some places strong winds blow in spring, summer, and fall, too.

Boom! How can you keep safe if you see lightning or hear thunder?

Talk about the words the author uses. Which words tell that bad weather is on its way?

Circle the words.

Write about these words.

Whoosh! is the sound of

_____

- -

_____

Boom! is the sound of

_____

- -

_____

Quick Tip

Words like *Whoosh!* and *Boom!* sound like what they mean.

Talk About It

Look at the Safety Kit checklist on page 32. Why does the author show this checklist? Talk about other things you can put in a safety kit.

Stormy Weather

Step 1 Talk about ways to stay safe in bad weather.
Choose one kind of bad weather to learn about.

Step 2 Write a question about how to stay safe
in this kind of weather.

_____

- -

_____

- -

_____

Step 3 Look at books or use the Internet.
Look up words you do not know.
Use a picture dictionary.

Step 4 **Write** a list of safety tips you learned.

_____

- -

_____

- -

_____

- -

_____

Step 5 **Choose** a good way to present your work.

_____

- -

_____

Talk about how this family stays safe and warm. What might the weather be like outside?

 Compare this photo with the ending of *Waiting Out the Storm*.

Quick Tip

We can talk about cold weather using these words:

chilly, freezing, frosty, icy, snowy, wintry

Goodshoot/Getty Images

What I Know Now

Think about the texts you read this week.

The texts tell about

_____

- -

_____

- -

_____

 Think about what you learned this week.
What else would you like to learn?
Talk about your ideas.

 Share one thing you learned about
realistic fiction stories.

Writing and Grammar

I wrote a realistic fiction story. Realistic fiction has characters who act like real people.

Pedro

Student Model

Camping Inside

Min is sad because it is raining.

She cannot go camping.

Min cannot sleep outside in a tent.

Realistic Fiction
My story has a character and events that could be real.

Then Min has a great idea.

Min puts old blankets over a table.

"I can go camping inside!"

Genre Study

 Talk about what makes Pedro's story realistic fiction.

 Circle who the story is about.

 Underline one event.

Plan

 Talk about ideas and characters for a realistic fiction story.

 Draw your story idea.

Quick Tip

Think about characters and events that could be real.

Write the name of your character.

_____

- -

_____

Write about an event.

_____

- -

_____

_____

- -

_____

Draft

Read Pedro's draft
of his realistic fiction story.

I organized my
story in a way
that makes sense.

A Rainy Day

Min is sad because it is raining.

Min cannot go camping.

Min cannot sleep outside in a tent

FXQuadro/Shutterstock.com

Plot: Sequence
I put the events in order.

Then Min has an idea.

Min puts old blankets over a table.

"I can go camping inside!"

 Your Turn

Begin to write your realistic fiction story in your writer's notebook. Use your ideas from pages 76–77.

Revise and Edit

Think about how Pedro revised and edited his writing.

I wrote a better title.

Student Model

Camping Inside

Min is sad because it is raining.

I changed *Min* to the **pronoun** *She*.

She cannot go camping.

Min cannot sleep outside in a tent.

I added an end mark.

FXQuadro/Shutterstock.com

- A **singular noun** names one thing.

- A **plural noun** names more than one thing.

- A **pronoun** can take the place of a noun.

I added a detail.

Then Min has a great idea.

Min puts old blankets over a table.

"I can go camping inside!"

I made sure to use a **plural** and **singular noun**.

Your Turn

Revise and edit your writing. Be sure to use singular and plural nouns and a pronoun. Use your checklist.

Share and Evaluate

 Practice presenting your work with a partner. Take turns.

 Present your work. Then use this checklist.

Sharing My Work	Yes	No
Writing and Grammar		
I wrote a realistic fiction story.	☐	☐
I wrote about a character who acts like a real person.	☐	☐
I used singular and plural nouns.	☐	☐
I used a pronoun.	☐	☐
Speaking and Listening		
I used correct grammar when I spoke.	☐	☐
I listened carefully.	☐	☐
I answered questions. I used details.	☐	☐

Talk with a partner about your writing.

Write about your work.

What did you do well in your writing?

_____

- -

_____

- -

_____

What do you need to work on?

_____

- -

_____

◎ Spiral Review

Genre
- Fantasy
- Nursery Rhyme
- Nonfiction

Skill
- Plot: Sequence
- Rhyme and Rhythm
- Main Topic/Key Details

Focus on Fantasy

A fantasy is a story with made-up characters, settings, or events.

 Listen to "Spring Is Here!"

 Talk about how you know this is a fantasy story.

 Write about the plot. What happens **first**, **next**, and **last**?

First

Next

Last

Focus on Nursery Rhymes

A **nursery rhyme** is a short poem for children that was written long ago.

 Listen to "Rain, Rain, Go Away."

 Talk about words in the poem that rhyme.

Rain, Rain, Go Away

Rain, rain, go away.

Come again some other day.

Rain, rain, go away.

Little children want to play.

Draw a picture of a word that rhymes with **day**.

 Listen to the poem again. Clap to the rhythm as you listen.

 Say the poem with a partner as you clap to the rhythm.

Talk About It

Talk about how a nursery rhyme is different from a story.

Focus on Nonfiction

Nonfiction text can have a **main topic**. The **key details** describe and tell more about the topic.

 Listen to "All Kinds of Trees." Think about what makes this text nonfiction.

 Talk about the main topic.

 Write the main topic.

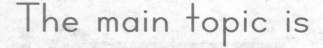 The main topic is

_____

- -

_____

Draw two key details that tell about the main topic.

1.

2.

Extend Your Learning

Reading Digitally

Online texts have special features, or **links**. You can click on these links to learn more.

 Listen to "Changes with the Wind." Ask your teacher to click on the links.

 Talk about what happens when you click on the first link.

 Write about the last link. What information does it tell?

_____

- -

_____

 Share something you learned.

Wind at Work

People can use the wind in different ways.

Talk about a question you have
about ways people can use the wind.

Decide where to find information
to answer your question. Do research.

Write the answer to your question.

_____

- -

_____

_____

- -

_____

 Share the information you learned.

Choose Your Own Book

 Write the title of the book.

 Tell a partner why you want to read it. Then read the book.

Minutes I Read

 Write your opinion of the book.

What Did You Learn?

Think about the skills you have learned.
How do you feel about what you can do?

 Circle a picture in each row.

I understand plot and what happens first, next, and last.	🙂	😐	🙁
I understand rhyme and rhythm.	🙂	😐	🙁
I understand main topic and key details.	🙂	😐	🙁

 Talk with a partner about a skill you want to get better at.

My Sound-Spellings

Aa a — apple

Bb b — bat

Cc c ck k — camel

Dd d — dolphin

Ee e — egg

Ff f — fire

Gg g — guitar

Hh h_ — hippo

Ii i — insect

Jj j — jump

Kk c k ck — koala

Ll l — lemon

Mm m — map

Nn n — nest

Oo o — octopus

Pp p — piano

Qq qu_ — queen

Rr r — rose

Ss s — sun

Tt t — turtle

Uu u — umbrella

Vv v — volcano

Ww w_ — window

Xx x — box

Yy y_ — yo-yo

Zz z _s — zipper